GROWING PAINS

BENJAMEN KILGORE

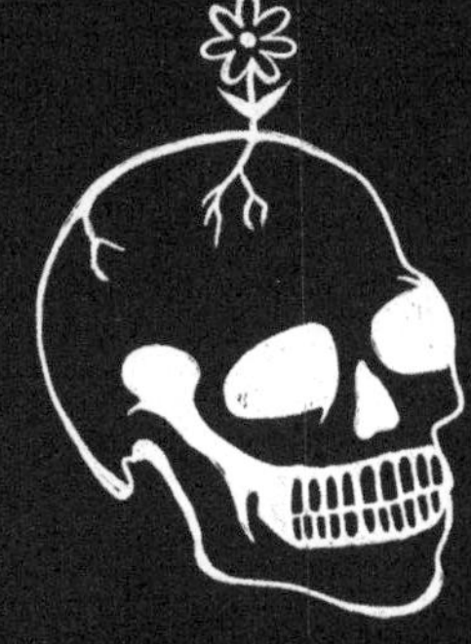

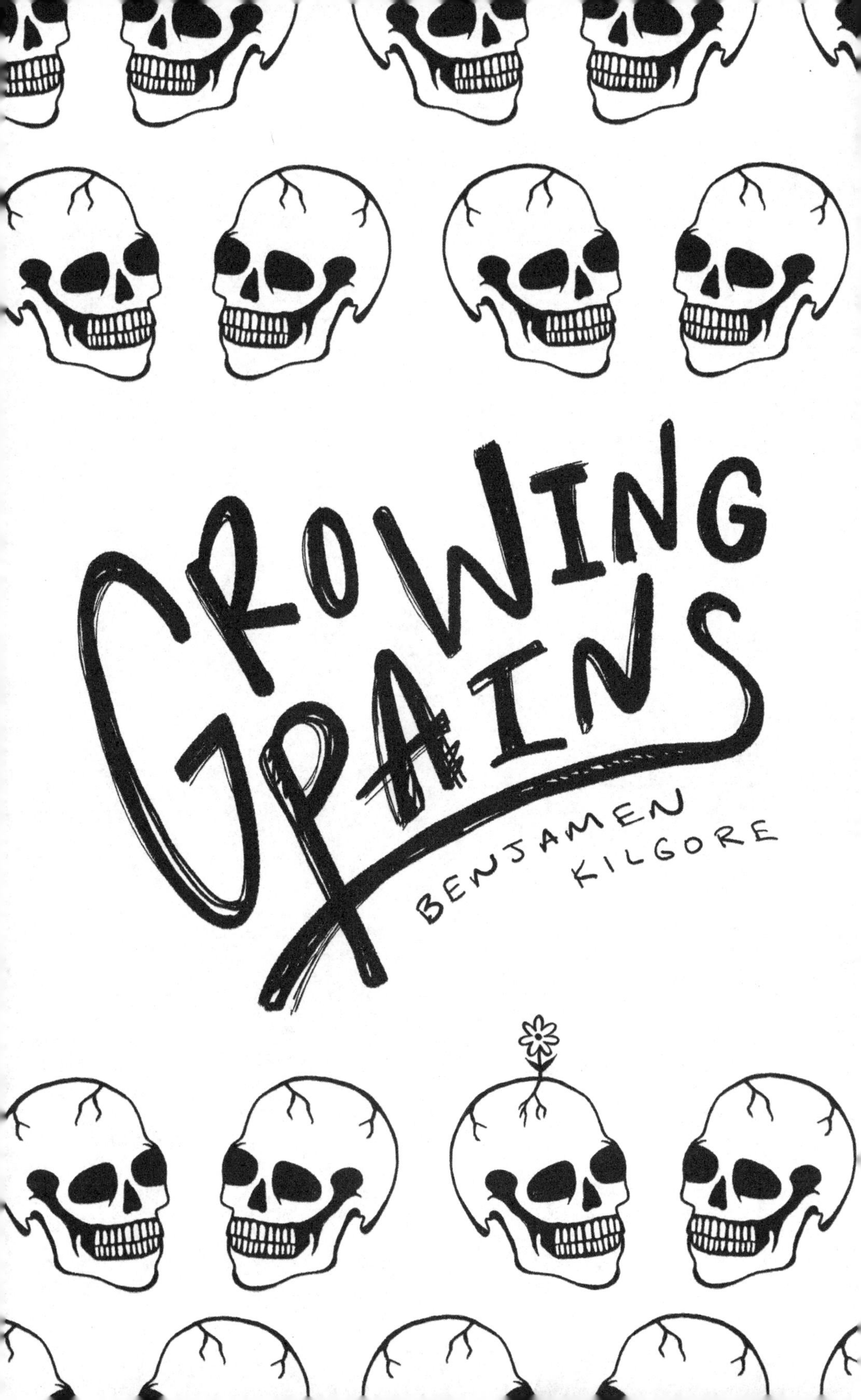
GROWING PAINS
BENJAMEN KILGORE

First paperback edition July 2020

Illustrations by Megan Kilgore

ISBN 9780578724324

@benjamenkilgore

FOR MEGAN

WHO MAKES EVERYTHING BRIGHTER.

CONTENTS

Careful now, dear Reader.
in your hands is
a portion of soul.
I am scared for you to hold it.

It ripped loose
from the rest
and I thought
it would kill me.

In its
brokenness
it is
whole.

Now I see
this piece
was always meant
to be yours.

There are two types of
growing pains:

There are the shin splints
the skinned knees
And the consequences of
Broken things.

Then there's the soul tearing
the heartbreaking
And the consequences of
Broken being.

The difference between the two:

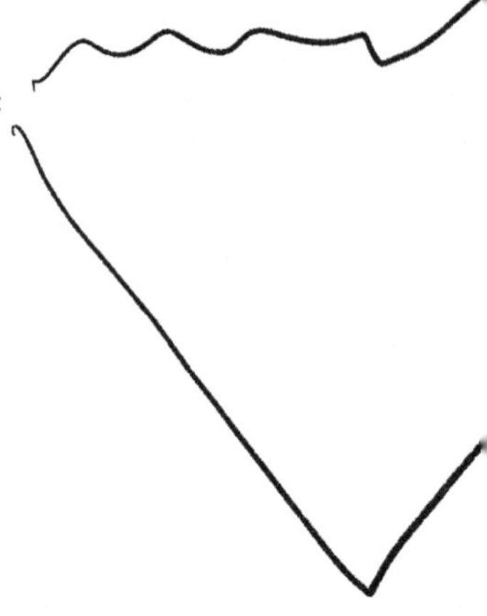

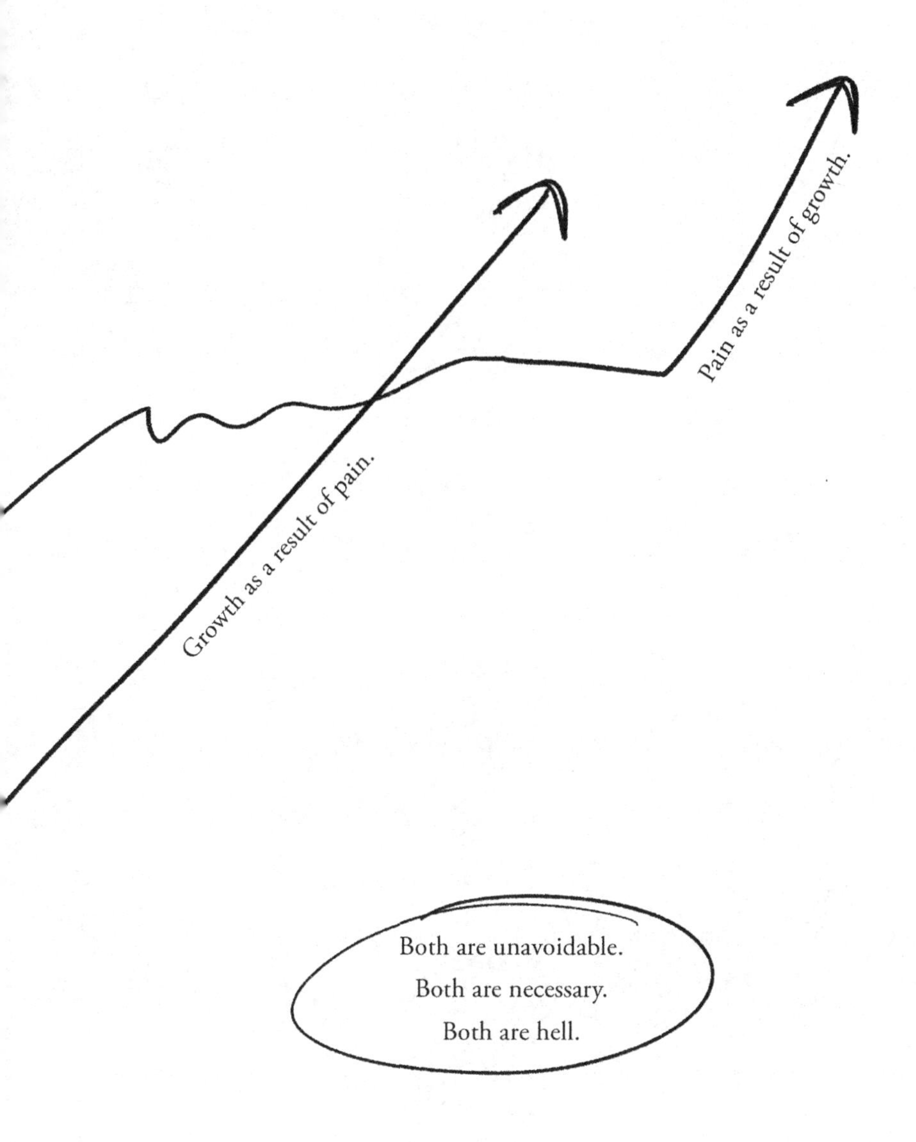
Growth as a result of pain.
Pain as a result of growth.
Both are unavoidable.
Both are necessary.
Both are hell.

P A

I N

I feel drawn to

the broken things;

the fallen birds

the chipped cups

torn books and

abandoned dreams.

Because maybe if I can

fix them

they can finally

fix me.

I can hear Today
yap and squeal
classic case of little-dog syndrome
with puffed chest and raised hair
drool hanging off the tiny canines.

Tomorrow is right behind him waiting
just waiting
on haunched legs ready
to pounce
to bloody
to feast
to feel the hope fade.

Neither of them get my attention
the delirious fools
Yesterday has me claimed
I can feel him gaining
can feel his breath
can feel him at my back.

I can feel him.

I used to believe that
cliches were dramatic
over-the-top
until I felt the secret take root.

Then I spent two hours
in the shower scrubbing
myself clean working down
the layers of skin to purify
the dirty blood.

I met you at your house
after I dropped off my prom date.
I couldn't look at her
couldn't see her.
All I thought about was you.

You opened your door
pressed your body against mine.
My handsome man
you whispered
to a seventeen-year-old
boy.

A whiff sent
my mind reeling
even after all this time.

Everytime I catch
the scent of your perfume
I smell the dried blood swirling beneath.

Cuddled close

intertwined like an

anaconda with its meal

you leaned in and breathed

God told me you were

my husband

and kissed me.

I thought God

must've told you

because I wasn't

good enough to hear for myself.

Did the rot come through

or maybe some ash

possibly a thick

sick phlegm

in the back of the throat

when you used

the voice of God

to trap me in hell?

God spoke to you
through you
and no one else.
If I ever strained
a sentence from Him
and set it at your feet
my sacrifice was wrong
or incomplete.

When I found you out
as a false prophet
a corrupt fool
was when
I first doubted God.

I prayed

fasted

repented of sins

covered by the blood years ago

to get the certainty you had.

I wanted to hear for myself.

When I got nothing but the

quiet

I attributed it to my shame.

Now I know I was listening

to the wrong one.

To be as sure as you

I should've been begging hell.

You gave me my fair share

in due season.

Before you told me about
the dreams
the vision
the prophecies
you messaged me
we can't do this

That tells me
the first thing you heard
was no.

UNHOLY TRINITY

You confessed your past
losing your virginity
getting wasted
and all the shame
as if I were a priest.

Searching to gain
affirmation
confirmation
affection
as if I were God.

You touched me
trained me
corrupted me
as if I were a pet.

And I
being a good boy
took it all
trading your sin
for my innocence.

You led me to your room
laid me down on your bed
played *Tangled.*
Just watch
you said
it has so many
supernatural truths
about God.

Then you cuddled
close
and slipped your
marshmallow hands
into my soul.

Dimmed lights

stereo humming

engine running

you want to kiss me

don't you

I nodded

Then what are you

waiting for

We kissed for the first time.

Then you shoved your tongue

in my left ear and threw your voice

live as an echo

in my skull

forever.

While worship was happening

we sat in the back

in the dark

as close as we could

without drawing

suspicion.

You stretched your pinky over

the gap in the chair

interlocking it with mine

our own pinky swear

that we will

NEVER

forget each other.

You picked the skin
from the bone
plucked the heart
from between the ribs
tore the soul
from the spirit
and left me
a skeleton boy
claiming my favorite parts
as blemished.

Reassembled
Reconstructed
Rebuilt

into your own
perverted image.

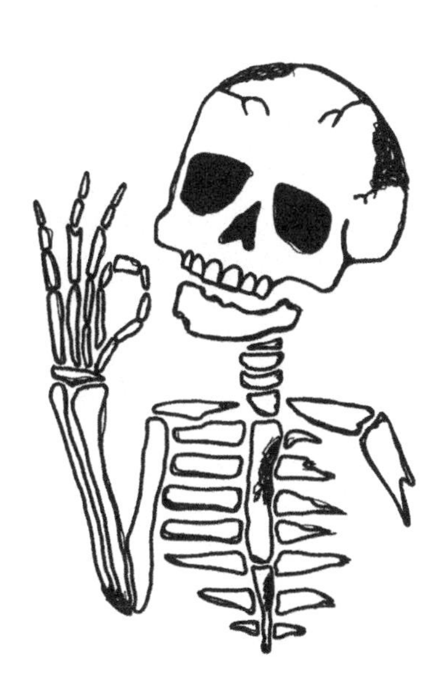

Sitting in the dark
you coached me on
how
and
when
to touch.

Ssssmall movementmentssss
you taught
Yessssss
you ssssaid
Jussssst like that.

Now I dream of cleaving
off my hands.
I don't want
the same trained fingers
used near my bride.

YOU'LL ALWAYS HAVE A PIECE OF ME

I dreamed of dancing hands

attached to arms

that fought every movement

and tried to get their act together

stop dancing and get it together

but they danced all the more

until I cut them off

at the wrist watching them

twirl away straight to you.

Deep in my chest
an egg hatched
and a squirming began
flowing in my veins
bubbling through the
underneath skin
against the pores

I felt the secret claim me
cacoon me
when you said
You told too many people about us.
People I didn't want to know.

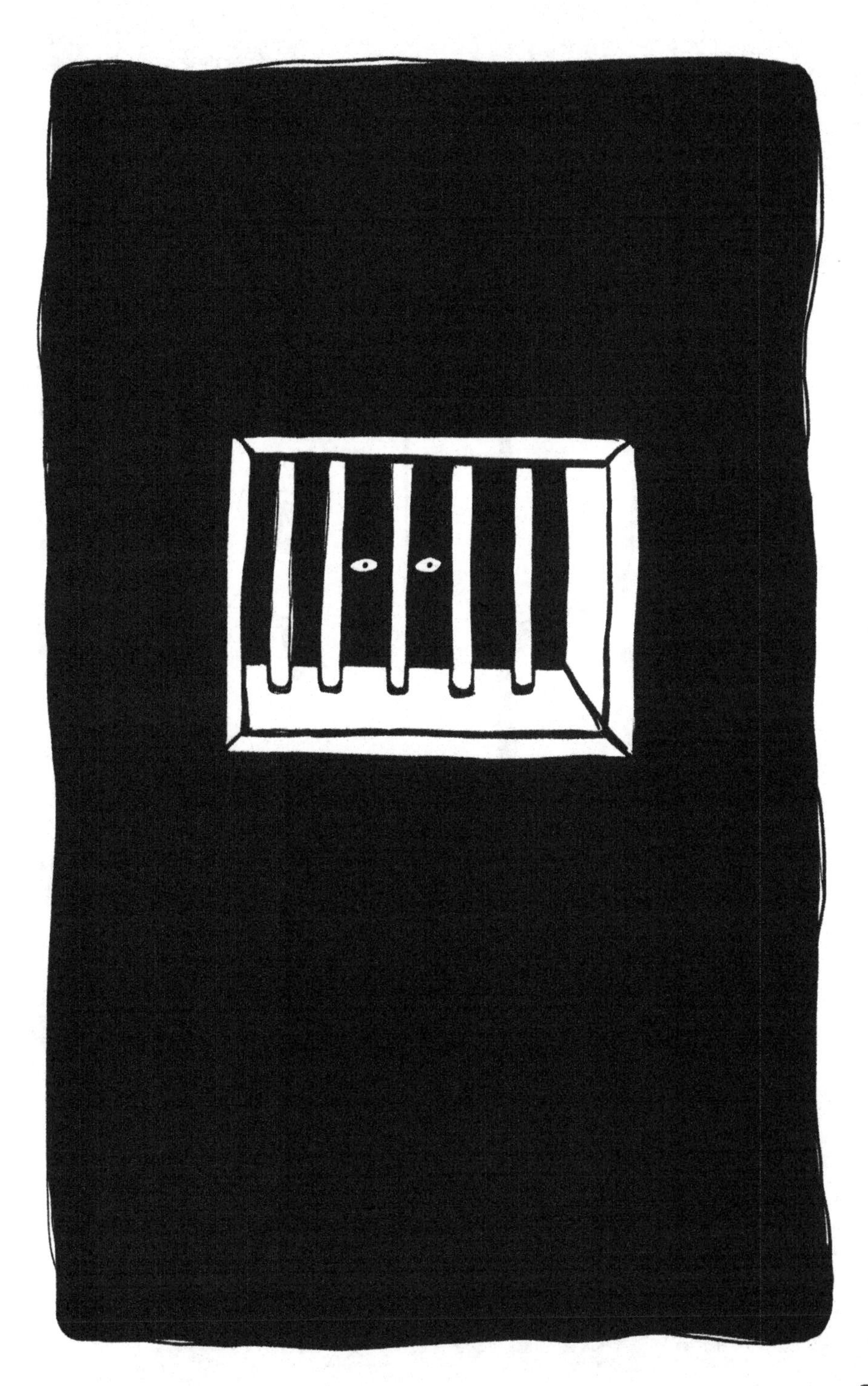

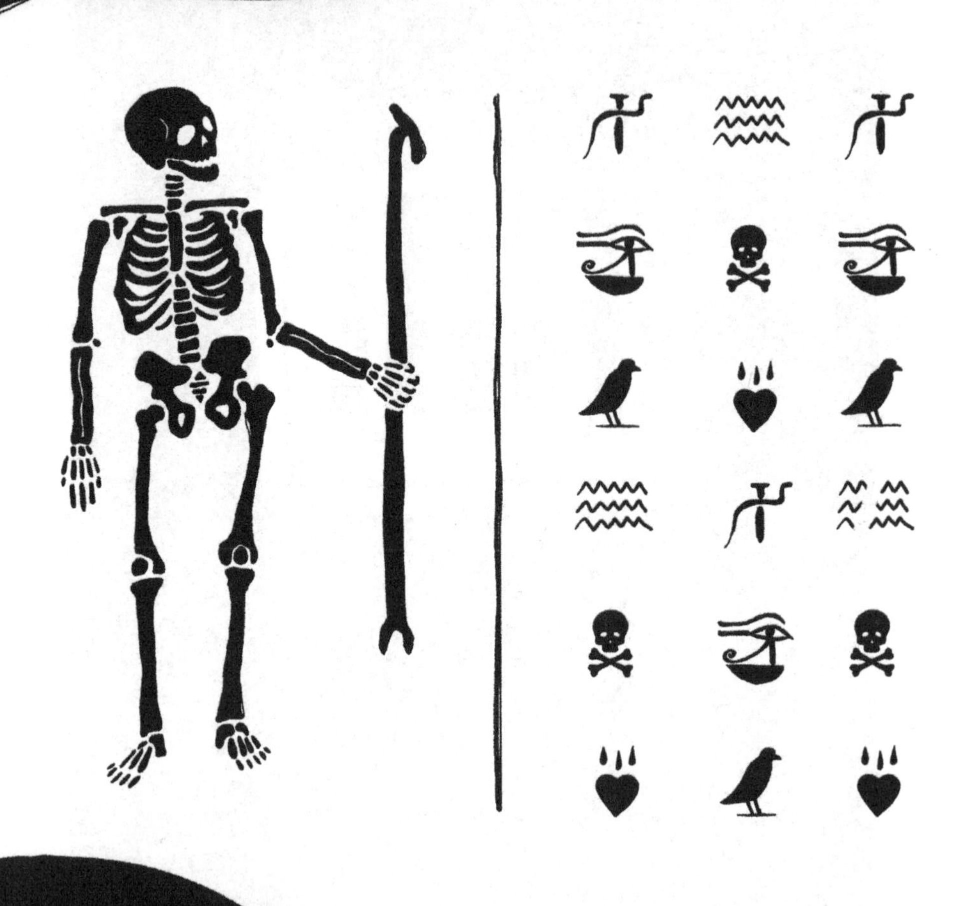

You are now married

with a daughter

your life uninterrupted

marching on into

the promised land

I am stuck to live

in this year

over and over

Egypt free of me

I'm slaved to Egypt

A year after we were finished,
-but let's be real we are never really finished are we-
while I had to hide from
pastors and parents and peers
because I was sure they could see
the sin on my skin
marked like Cain
for everyone to see
and they had better not
get close
or something seven times worse
would happen to them
and their children,
you started dating your husband.
Did you tell him about me?

WILL YOU TEACH

YOUR DAUGHTER TO

LOOK OUT FOR

EVERYTHING YOU WERE?

I PRAY SHE

TAKES NOTES AND

NEVER SUFFERS FROM

SOMEONE LIKE YOU.

EXTRA, EXTRA

The news had broken
blistering light scolding
with eyes that shouted
you should've known better
and the light was so
-what's the word?-
heavy
-I think-
that I felt all my bones
were dust crushed
by the
-oh come on-
weight yes weight
and the last thing
to go was my ability to
-wait what was I saying-
to think.

And when I finally broke
those who I believed to help
put my bones back together
rushed in to scatter
the pieces and silence
the one slowing up the pack

The ground opened beneath

spewed red lava around me and

swallowed me

starting with the hands

a scarlet scar in the earth of my soul

where hell had a firm grip and

some ripe soul to grow and grow.

FAMILIARITY

I didn't die in a moment.

I died slowly.

I died everyday.

I chose it.

DARK THOUGHTS

I dream of hurting myself

hurling my body down flights of stairs

driving into the concrete barricade.

I don't want to die

just a reason to feel nothing

a reason to feel how I do.

My head is full of mashed potatoes
whipped to a lovely winter fog
slowly drip-drop-dripping
out my ears eyes nose mouth
seeping oozing filtering
pressing tight against
my thin skin
and escaping out every pore
in a pulsated flow
of liquified brain tissue

I try to capture it
with a homemade net
but it sifts between the cracks
like sand courses through your hands
not wet sand but the dry kind
you find in your shoes
after a day at the beach

but my mind is more like
wet sand plopped between my ears
in a skullish aquarium
showing the sloshing and swishing
against bone walls that eroded away
long ago and don't care how high

the sea of thoughts tide
grows because we already know they can see.

Oh yes. They can see my head full of foggy wet sand potatoes.

The doctor called it depression.

I'm just a skeleton boy

with skeleton fingers

spitting into the dirt

and making mud

trying to make

new flesh.

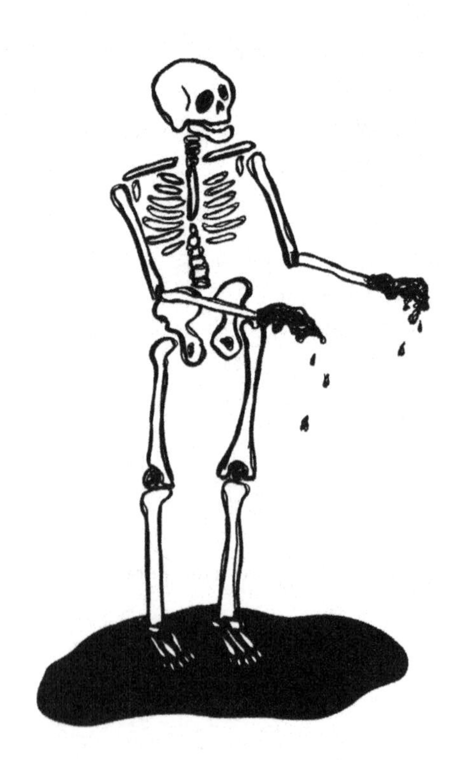

When it was over
-at least over to you-
you were convinced
that all that was
necessary for
healing
was
forgiveness.

But in order to
forgive
one must have
a soul.

So there you are
holding my soul for ransom
at the cost of my forgiveness.

You just need to forgive her

they said.

Look her in the eye

and forgive her.

I wonder how well

they would stand

looking into the eyes

of their custom evil.

IT'S BEEN SEVEN YEARS

Fear rises and a cold sweat breaks

the feeling of a tiger prowling

in the tall grass just out before me

as I look at my phone and see

after all this time

you like my old posts.

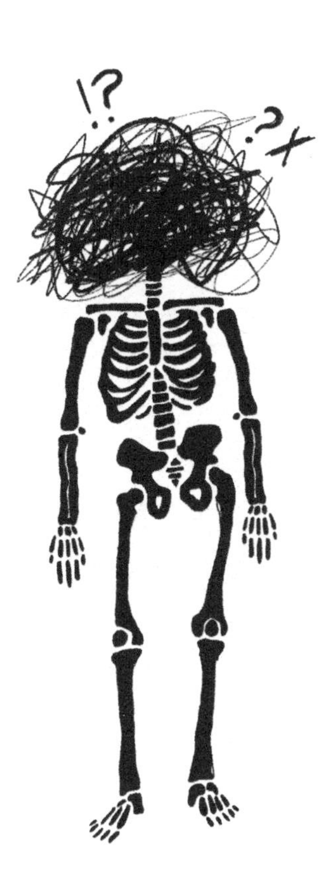

There are two types of fire:
the red and the black.

Red is light and inviting
offering to burn away
all the infirmities and insecurities

Black has no hope of heat.

You used my bones as flint
and lit a black fire
that wasn't content
till I was consumed.

AFTER THE FIRE HAD BEGUN TO TAKE ME

IT WAS THE ONES I THOUGHT WOULD

PULL ME UP

AND

PUT ME OUT

THAT REPOSITIONED ME SO I CAN BURN

EVENLY.

THE FEEL OF FALLING FURTHER INTO BEING FORGOTTEN

WAS THE ONLY FEELING LEFT.

Maybe I deserve this
I thought
Maybe this is my fault
I said
I did kiss her back
I reasoned

that's when I learned
shame begins
as a question

You took my raw clay
and fashioned me
into your deepest secret
an ornate misery.

Like a good secret
I kept to the
dark things
and let the
black flame
engulf me
set me
solidify me.

Bones hallowed and dried
of all marrow and life
reframed to be an altar for you
to sacrifice to burn whatever
evidence of innocence was left.

When the pyre took

and the fire claimed me

I got lost in the wonder

of how bright I was.

THE FIRE DIED AND I

WAS LEFT MY OWN

ASH-MADE MONSTER

TO LINGER IN THE NIGHT.

I stood in the ashen dark

forgotten and wounded

and that's when I heard

the whispers of the grave

promising to bind me up

and make all the pain go away.

All that was required was

everything

written in blood.

I could hear further in the dark

the dead part of me

the ghoul of the

rotten sacrifice

whisper to me with

its rose voice

and beckon me with

its lemon scent.

So I lingered in

further

than ever dreamed

chasing the ghost of me.

SECRETS THRIVE IN THE DARK

SO I STOOD BACK

AND LISTENED INTENTLY

TO THE VOID.

Crows as big as the night itself

would pick and claw at my skin and bone

taking chunks of soul back to build their home.

They drew the blood

and drank it in full

and I no longer care.

FILLED WITH MURDER

The crows feasted on flesh

till they picked me dry

and they weren't content

so they went inside

through my wounds and mouth

and rearranged the organs

reconstructed the bones

to build their nest.

SHADOW GIANTS

In life they thum and thump
towering over all with
their magnificent height
with no real opponent
but they eventually fall.

When they die their
massiveness
is converted to
nothingness
and there is nothing quite
as suffocating as
nothingness.

Their shade is morphed
into the very air
making every breath
full of horror and pain
until the giant makes
his home in you.

Slain giants create
the most haunting of ghosts.

Sometimes late in the blue
I spend my remaining waking
moments thinking of you
to try and ease the shaking
the falling into the pit
feeling your fingers in my soul
nails in my veins at that moment
is so much better than the cold

I pick at the red raw bumps
and scars beating with their own hearts
pounding and breaking with throbs and thumps
drawing blood from the tender spots

The antipathy
outweighs the empty.

Every now and again

when the air of nothing

is stale and suffocating

I'll pick and scratch

at the red scar

til some of the blood and shame

oozes out

to remind myself of feeling.

TRICKS I PICKED UP IN THERAPY

When confronted with your own monster
and you are certain he really has you
look in his bloody face with laughter
and as he pounces, laugh till you breakthrough

So I tried and faked a giggle
hoping to summon an authentic joy
as the migraines grew little by little
mind racing to remember what I enjoy

Fangs bared, the beast flew at me
and swallowed me crying
He didn't bother to see
how hard I was trying.

IT FELT GOOD TO BE ACCEPTED

Smothering, suffocating smoke surrounded

and subjected me bleeding inside

through the eyes and ears

and anywhere else it could sink

its biting in so deep to get

to the heart of me.

It nestled me

embraced me.

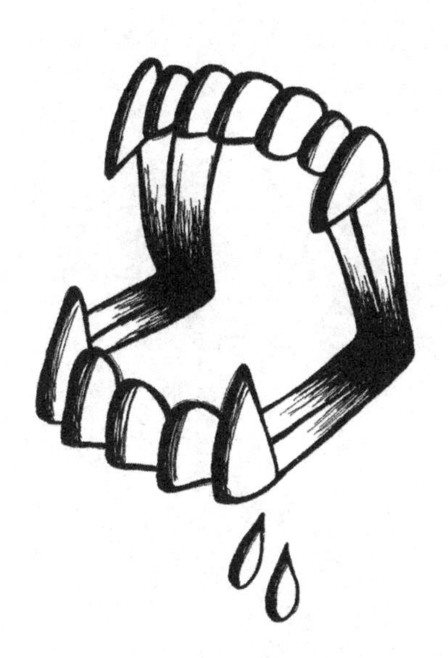

HA HA HA
HE HE HE...LP

PRACTICED LAUGHING

Cracked heels on a tiled floor

broken face staring back through

a foggy mirror with wrinkles stretched

across the forehead and down the sides

of each eye, gray hair peppered

through the unwashed brown

too young to have either

too tired to mind

laughing at the image

getting the pitch just right

working out the line between

believable and lunacy

squinting in disgust

when the smile

doesn't touch the eyes.

A remnant of you
lives and breathes
in every disappointment
I experience.

Every shameful moment
summons you like a
genie or crossroads
demon.

You were
my first
and none have
compared since.

The scariest things linger in the shadows

just beyond where the light ends

and in Sunday School

they don't tell about the end

but when

you're in the dark you

don't even know how scary

they are because you can't see them

only hear them

FALSE HOPE

Drunk off a bottle of Jack
attempting to distract my bitter
mind with something a little more
hoping that maybe if I pour enough
whiskey it'll drown like those
poor unrighteous souls who stared up
at Noah for salvation but they were
too little too late and
-oh stop crying-
they should've looked to God first
but they didn't and neither did I
so now I'm wasted on the fire
trying to forget but all it does is make me
remember

NIGHT CAP

I'D GET SO DRUNK THAT I NEVER REMEMBERED WHEN THE CRYING STARTED.

The first bottle of whiskey I drank

the mask slipped and the weight of shame

loosened for a second and I didn't care that I was exposed.

Then the drink faded along

with the pale light

leaving me deeper in the pit

than I had been before

and it was years before I gained

the sober strength

to take the mask off again.

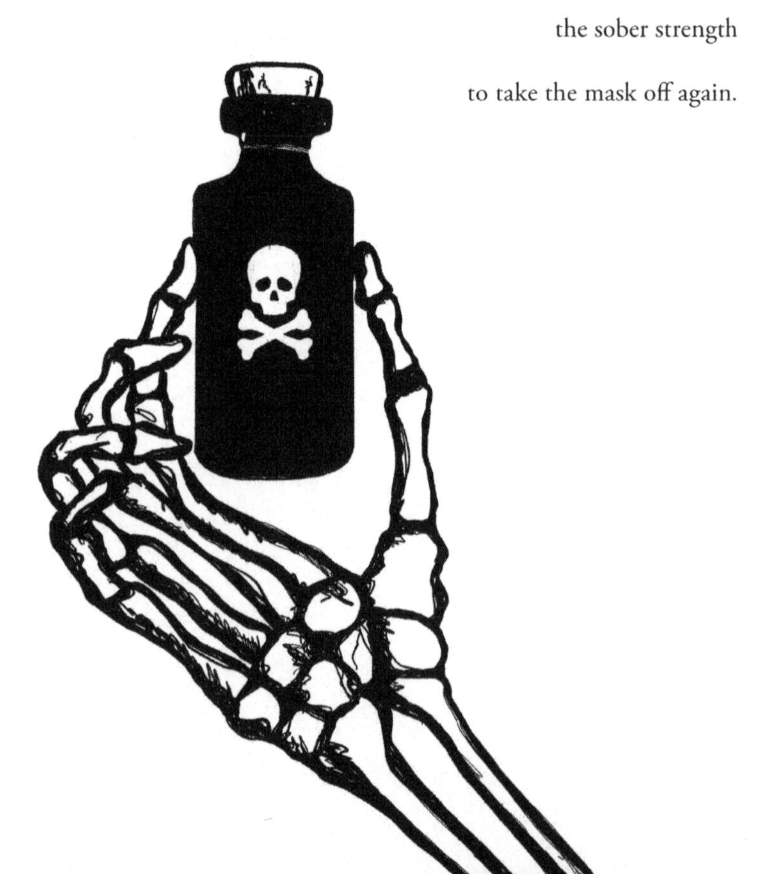

ROMANS 8:28

I sat with all my lights off
and whispered the promise
until I cried myself to sleep.

THE DARK SMOTHERED AND SEEPED

THROUGH THE PORES AND INHALES SO DEEP

THAT IT BECAME PART OF ME.

I made a home in the pit
chained to the past
to live and breathe the moment
when the light went out forever.

Just then, a
rushing
mighty
whisper
came and took my hands.

It broke the chains
loosened the shame
and walked me out.

Even when I fought to go back
for my things
for my self
it urged me onward
into the day.

G R O

W T H

ACT OF BRAVERY

Pen shaking
sweat building
practiced breathing after every word
in-and-out
two-more-times
(jusssst-like-thatttt)
heart pounding, raging against
the pen, calling it a coward
for ratting us out.
What will they think?
(what will you think?)
Mind racing now
searching for a way out
but the pen marches on.

HERE
was
LIES A
BOY

In the bright day I can finally see
how deep the wounds go
how far they reach.
They ooze and stink
green pus and bile
a waterfall of infection
that cascades
down the ribcage
and weaves
through the veins
and drowns the
wanderers
who get
a little too
lost.

The secret still writhed
and thrashed in the light
I could feel it in my chest
with its fangs in my heart
pumping poison in my soul.

The first time I told
my story was to myself
even then I could feel it
loosen, shift, fracture.

I could sense that deeper
some forgotten piece
the human piece
began breathing shallow breaths.

The tenth time the secret shriveled
wrapped around itself and rattled
at the danger of exposure.

That forgotten part grew more
until it was
a distant memory filled
with fog and uncertainty.

The hundredth time the remembered part
rooted in my soul
lobbed the head off the secret serpent
and threw it out of my mouth and into the light.

DRY BONES

Pieces of me littered in the pit
aimlessly dropped, chipped and scattered
throughout the black plains
marking my journey
like bread crumbs.
They began rattling and shaking
and I can feel them,
every piece,
twitch and flail and roll.
They shot through the black
and into the light
back to me,
joints to sockets,
marrow to bone,
blood to veins.

THE DOVE AND THE CROWS

The crows were still home
in the marrow of my bones
even in the broad sunlight.
I could hear their clicks and caws,
feel their hooked feet around the heart,
could sense those soulless eyes
piercing through the skin.

Then a dove,
gentle and wild,
descended and landed on my shoulder.
The crows raged festered,
anchored to their nest
and they'd be damned before they left.

But the dove stood silent, strong.

The black wings cut like razors
slicing in their frenzy
and I couldn't stand it any longer.

Just when I thought of driving the dove away,
the crows released
and flew out of their roost
and into the open air.

The dove dove from his perch
and swallowed them whole.

Caught between
who I was
and
who I'm becoming,
stuck on the line of
shame
and
purpose,
learning to knit
the two together.

There's a ghost living within me.
He is ancient and unmoving
flowing through the marrow and blood
sifting through the dead parts
He rebuilds the decaying things
destroying the foundation
I considered necessary.
Now I am fractured and he likes that
He is an old ghost
I am a new one.

The dark made it hard to

move

think

be.

All the ingredients

to being human.

I CLUNG TO MY WOUNDS

ENSNARED MY HURT

LIKE THE DARK CLINGS

TO CORNERS AND NOOKS

AND TO THE MINDS OF THE CRUEL

THINKING ITS WHAT

MADE ME HUMAN.

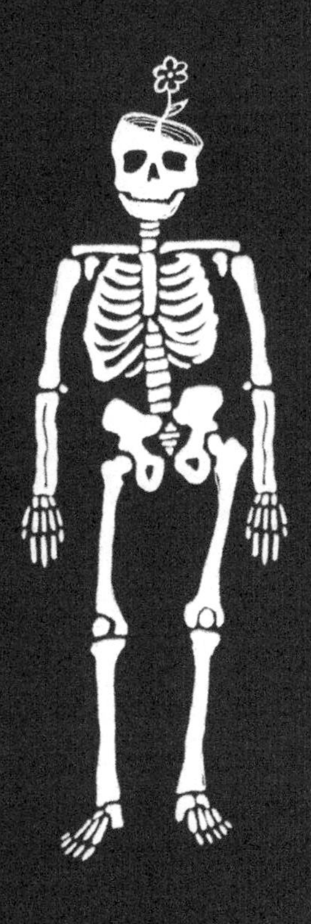

A Red fire sits on my chest

and seeps through my pores

into my heart

It was a violent thing

and I shook so hard that

I broke.

Or was I

already broken?

The fire doesn't care

He keeps burning, torching.

I do not mind

I love the feeling of dying

while being wholly alive.

I believed that my only way
to feel was through my hurt
so I tied it around my ribs
and tucked it in my heart
because feeling pain
is better than nothing.

But my pain lied.
It only sought to
make me lesser
make me weaker
make me beg.

OH! To be human again!
Before I was an ashen beast
filled with poison and pain
made to fit in places
never designed to go.

OH! To be human again!
Without the plastered clay
and glued on mud
pretending to be a real boy
hoping it to be true.

OH! To be human again!
To feel the warm breath
on a renewed soul
on a restored flesh
say *it is very good.*

OH! To be human again!
Anything less is hell.

The black stripped

and scraped every piece

of individuality

every trace of being human

moving in and out of the souls

of the huddled mass

whispering the chants to be sung

the words to be recited

in hushed and hoarse voices

we repeated and repeated.

The light gave me my voice back.

I laugh more now
and much harder
than any of my years
spent in the dark.
I'm amazed by the ease of it.

The dark still calls my name

from time to time

and the part of me that

likes comfort urges me

to go back and nestle up

but I've learned to

live again

and I'll rot before

I go back.

The shadows still pass
from time to time
but they don't stay long
since I've started seeing
the light behind them

I remember
having to ask myself
grounding questions
(where am I)
(what am I doing here)
(what is my name)
(where is she)
and sometimes I didn't know
the answers
and the grounding questions would
bury me.

I remember those moments
and I can see
the questions
floating in your eyes.

Come now
all you abandoned
all you lost
all you forgotten.

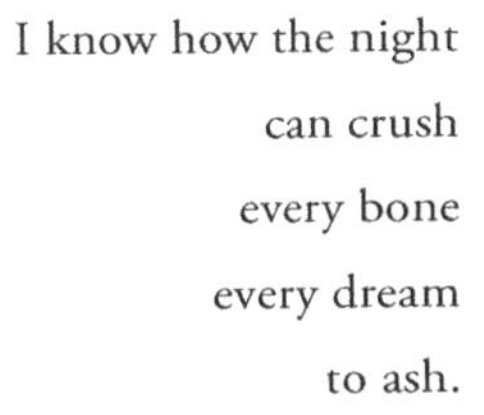

I know how the night
can crush
every bone
every dream
to ash.

I know the ache
down in the soul
for a glimpse of the end.

Listen
can you hear it?

Draw close.
The dawn is breaking.
The night is over.

:)

I thought of you today
for the first time
in a long time.
I thought of
your family
your friends.
I thought of
jokes you tell
movies you enjoy
life you live.

I thought of you today
and I hope you are better.

The things that used to

smother me

keep me pinned

are just passing thoughts now.

Redemption isn't always

a glorious moment

but the climax

of common ones.

I always expected

the triumphant moment

after the glorious battle,

the yell of victory

after the mesmerizing fight,

to be the sign of wholeness.

Instead, it was the mundane

everyday

common

and

constant

moving forward.

The blank pages

in the notebooks around me

are no longer condemning.

I feel no shame

flipping through

the empty spaces.

They are calling out

asking where I've been.

I can hardly wait to tell them.

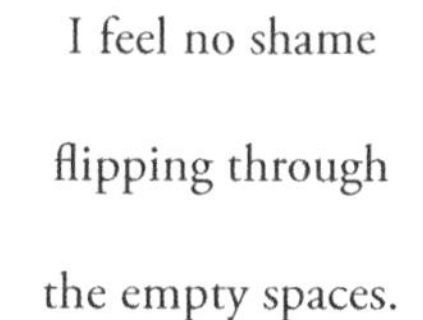

Now that the air is clear
the sun is out
I'll tell you all the things
I was dying to hear
when I was lost
and alone
not sure when
(if)
I would feel again.

I hope you sitting
in the pit I called home
can hear this through
the echoing shame
the thundering guilt
the deafening isolation
and know
I understand.

Wherever you are

in whatever state

you might be

write it down.

One day you'll read it

and weep with joy.

You have more fight in you

than you'll allow yourself to feel.

FIGHT DIRTY

Q(*.*Q)

If you want to get out
and you will need to decide that for
yourself
you need to fight like hell
because anything less than that
just won't work.

Roll your sleeves up.
Get a fistful of sand.
Stick razors in the gloves.
FIGHT DIRTY.

The stars were made

for each and every one of us

for the moments when

we find the dark too much.

THAT BLAZING STAR

HOVERING OVER THE MANGER

LED THOSE WHO SOUGHT

DIRECTLY TO HIM.

THERE'S A STAR

LINGERING OVER YOU.

PEOPLE ARE LOOKING.

JUST WAIT.

There is a you-sized hole
in the heart and soul
of this world
and we've tried to fill it
but nothing compares to you.

When you're ready
when you step into it
you won't lack anything
it won't be any lesser.

You'll be surprised
by how well you fit.

AS A SECRET. I WAS FAR MORE COMFORTABLE AS A SECRET. I WAS FAR MORE C
I WAS FAR MORE COMFORTABLE AS A SECRET. I WAS FAR MORE COMFORTABLE A
COMFORTABLE AS A SECRET. I WAS FAR MORE COMFORTABLE AS A SECRET. I W
AS A SECRET. I WAS FAR MORE COMFORTABLE AS A SECRET. I WAS FAR MORE C
I WAS FAR MORE COMFORTABLE AS A SECRET. I WAS FAR MORE COMFORTABLE A
COMFORTABLE AS A SECRET. I WAS FAR MORE COMFORTABLE AS A SECRET. I W
AS A SECRET. I WAS FAR MORE COMFORTABLE AS A SECRET. I WAS FAR MORE C
I WAS FAR MORE COMFORTABLE AS A SECRET. I WAS FAR MORE COMFORTABLE A
COMFORTABLE AS A SECRET. I WAS FAR MORE COMFORTABLE AS A SECRET. I W
AS A SECRET. I WAS FAR MORE COMFORTABLE AS A SECRET. I WAS FAR MORE C
I WAS FAR MORE COMFORTABLE AS A SECRET. I WAS FAR MORE COMFORTABLE A
COMFORTABLE AS A SECRET. I WAS FAR MORE COMFORTABLE AS A SECRET. I W
SECRET. **I WAS FAR MORE COMFORTABLE AS A SECRET.** *I W*
I WAS FAR MORE COMFORTABLE AS A SECRET. I WAS FAR MORE COMFORTABLE A
COMFORTABLE AS A SECRET. I WAS FAR MORE COMFORTABLE AS A SECRET. I W
AS A SECRET. I WAS FAR MORE COMFORTABLE AS A SECRET. I WAS FAR MORE C
I WAS FAR MORE COMFORTABLE AS A SECRET. I WAS FAR MORE COMFORTABLE A
COMFORTABLE AS A SECRET. I WAS FAR MORE COMFORTABLE AS A SECRET. I W
AS A SECRET. I WAS FAR MORE COMFORTABLE AS A SECRET. I WAS FAR MORE C
I WAS FAR MORE COMFORTABLE AS A SECRET. I WAS FAR MORE COMFORTABLE A
COMFORTABLE AS A SECRET. I WAS FAR MORE COMFORTABLE AS A SECRET. I W
AS A SECRET. I WAS FAR MORE COMFORTABLE AS A SECRET. I WAS FAR MORE C
I WAS FAR MORE COMFORTABLE AS A SECRET. I WAS FAR MORE COMFORTABLE A
COMFORTABLE AS A SECRET. I WAS FAR MORE COMFORTABLE AS A SECRET. I W
AS A SECRET. I WAS FAR MORE COMFORTABLE AS A SECRET. I WAS FAR MORE C
I WAS FAR MORE COMFORTABLE AS A SECRET. I WAS FAR MORE COMFORTABLE A
COMFORTABLE AS A SECRET. I WAS FAR MORE COMFORTABLE AS A SECRET. I W
AS A SECRET. I WAS FAR MORE COMFORTABLE AS A SECRET. I WAS FAR MORE C
I WAS FAR MORE COMFORTABLE AS A SECRET. I WAS FAR MORE COMFORTABLE A
COMFORTABLE AS A SECRET. I WAS FAR MORE COMFORTABLE AS A SECRET. I W
AS A SECRET. I WAS FAR MORE COMFORTABLE AS A SECRET. I WAS FAR MORE C

BENJAMEN KILGORE

ALIVE AS A STORY. I BECAME FAR MORE ALIVE AS A STORY. I BECAME FAR MORE
AR MORE ALIVE AS A STORY. I BECAME FAR MORE ALIVE AS A STORY. I BECAME F
BECAME FAR MORE ALIVE AS A STORY. I BECAME FAR MORE ALIVE AS A STORY. I
STORY. I BECAME FAR MORE ALIVE AS A STORY. I BECAME FAR MORE ALIVE AS
ALIVE AS A STORY. I BECAME FAR MORE ALIVE AS A STORY. I BECAME FAR MORE
AR MORE ALIVE AS A STORY. I BECAME FAR MORE ALIVE AS A STORY. I BECAME F
BECAME FAR MORE ALIVE AS A STORY. I BECAME FAR MORE ALIVE AS A STORY. I
STORY. I BECAME FAR MORE ALIVE AS A STORY. I BECAME FAR MORE ALIVE AS
ALIVE AS A STORY. I BECAME FAR MORE ALIVE AS A STORY. I BECAME FAR MORE
AR MORE ALIVE AS A STORY. I BECAME FAR MORE ALIVE AS A STORY. I BECAME F
BECAME FAR MORE ALIVE AS A STORY. I BECAME FAR MORE ALIVE AS A STORY. I
STORY. I BECAME FAR MORE ALIVE AS A STORY. I BECAME FAR MORE ALIVE AS
STORY. **I BECAME FAR MORE ALIVE AS A STORY.** *I BECAME FA*
ALIVE AS A STORY. I BECAME FAR MORE ALIVE AS A STORY. I BECAME FAR MORE
AR MORE ALIVE AS A STORY. I BECAME FAR MORE ALIVE AS A STORY. I BECAME F
BECAME FAR MORE ALIVE AS A STORY. I BECAME FAR MORE ALIVE AS A STORY. I 
STORY. I BECAME FAR MORE ALIVE AS A BECAME FAR MORE ALIVE AS
ALIVE AS A STORY. I BECAME FAR MORE STORY. I BECAME FAR MORE
AR MORE ALIVE AS A STORY. I BECAME FA IVE AS A STORY. I BECAME F
BECAME FAR MORE ALIVE AS A STORY. I AR MORE ALIVE AS A STORY. I
STORY. I BECAME FAR MORE ALIVE AS A S I BECAME FAR MORE ALIVE AS
ALIVE AS A STORY. I BECA MORE A STORY. I BECAME FAR MORE
AR MORE ALIVE AS A BECAME FAR ORE E AS A STORY. I BECAME F
BECAME FAR MORE A STORY. I CAME FAR E ALIVE AS A STORY. I
STORY. I BECA FAR MORE ALIVE A A S ORY. I BECAME AR MORE ALIVE AS
ALIVE AS A STO ECAME FAR MORE ALI AS A STORY. I CAME FAR MORE
AR MORE ALIV ORY. I BECAME FAR MORE ALIVE A ORY. I BECAME F
BECAME FAR IVE AS A STORY. AS A STORY. I
STORY. I BE E FAR MORE ALIVE ECA ORE ALIVE AS
ALIVE AS A ST . I B MOR ST ME FAR MORE
AR MORE ALIV S A AME FA RE ALI A STO Y. I BECAME F

ABOUT THE AUTHOR

Benjamen Kilgore is originally from Houston, Texas, but now lives in Birmingham, Alabama. He is the son of James and Nancy Kilgore, brother to Bo and Lace Kilgore, uncle to Scarlett Joan and Imogene, and husband to Megan Kilgore. He graduated from University of North Texas with a BA in English - Creative Writing. He enjoys a nice cup of coffee and a good novel, and hopes that you are having a great day.

Made in the USA
Columbia, SC
06 August 2020

15647904R00065